HAITI: Contributions to the World

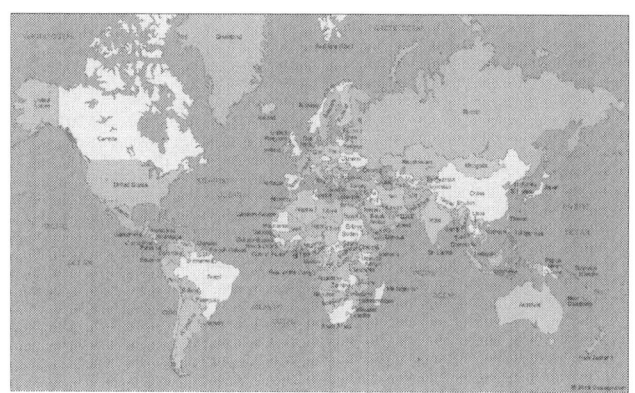

A COMPILATION OF HISTORICAL FACTS

JEAN PAUL JEAN FRANÇOIS

HAITI:
Contributions to the World

HAITI: Contributions to the World

JEAN PAUL JEAN FRANÇOIS
jpjf561@gmail.com

ISBN: 9781091586161

© Tous droits réservés 2019

Couverture : Éditions PerleDesAntilles
Mise en pages : Éditions PerleDesAntilles

Éditions PerleDesAntilles
7054 Chesapeake Circle
Boynton Beach, Florida 33436

Marin 12 # 7
Port-au-Prince, Haïti W.I.

perledesantilles1804@gmail.com

HAITI: Contributions to the World

Note

In French and English encyclopedias and dictionaries today, there is the island of Hispaniola divided into the countries of *Haiti* and the Dominican Republic. During my compilation work of historical facts about Haiti, I have discovered and reproduced two official documents with the original spelling of "Hayti": The Act of Independence and the Invitation Letter of Jean-Pierre Boyer to the African-Americans. Some reports stated that the new spelling "Haiti" was adopted in the 1930s when the Dominican Republic Geographic Board was urged by the Dominican Republic government to name or rename the entire island Hispaniola.

In this document, I will use "Hayti" for all the facts before the year of 1930 and "Haiti" for those after while I am still questioning when that change had become official by a Haytian government.

HAITI: Contributions to the World

CONTENTS

From the author..11
Acknowledgments...13
Foreword...15

Chapter I: Hayti/Haiti 's: Land – Population – Languages 17
              Hayti/Haiti, Pioneer of Freedom........................19

Chapter II: Hayti/Haiti 's Contributions to the North-American
              Countries..28

Chapter III: Hayti/Haiti 's Contributions to the Dominican
              Republic...59

Chapter IV: Hayti/Haiti 's contributions to the South and
              Central American Countries............................64

Chapter V: Hayti/Haiti's contributions to the European,
              African, and Middle-Eastern countries..............67

Chapter VI: Summary..75

Conclusion..78

Appendices: Historical pictures..80

FROM THE AUTHOR

I am neither a historian nor a social studies teacher; I am an Educator, Accountant, and a graduate in Electrical Engineering and Chemistry. As an educator and promotor of Haiti's culture and history in the United States, I have always been fascinated by the history of the world in general, particularly the great history of Hayti/Haiti, a small country that contributed to change the world in the late eighteenth to nineteenth century.

I have been educating others about the cultural and historic values of Haiti for the past eighteen years and have a desire to continue through this compilation of historical facts about Haiti's contributions to the World.

I hope that the compilation of these historical facts of Haiti's invaluable contributions to the world will make you aware of the great history of Haiti, pioneer of anti-slavery, anti-colonization and anti-segregation in the world.

ACKNOWLEDGMENTS

First, I have started and finished this compilation under the guidance of Engineer Agronomist Bito David, M.Ed., educator, writer and promotor of Haitian Heritage Month Celebration in Palm Beach County, Florida, USA. Golden Achievement Award recipient in 2005 for his dedicated work in promoting Haiti's contributions to the history of humanity, Bito David has been a mentor and role model to me for many years.

Secondly, over the last two years, I have spent a tremendous amount of time discussing history with Professor Abel Clervil, writer, militant in history and culture of Haiti. Abel Clervil is a historian who has been advocating against the distortion of historical facts about Haiti. Professor Clervil has contributed largely to my knowledge.

Lastly but not least, it was the enormous support of Rev. Wilson Depas, MBA, educator, a servant leader whose advices and encouragement fueled my desire to succeed in my work. I am very grateful to him for his continued support.

FOREWORD

This book is a compilation of the contributions of Haiti and its people to the world. A small country in area, a great nation in history, the first Black independent nation in the modern world, the history of Haiti has influenced the course of the history of many great nations.

From politics to economics, from social organizations to racial interactions, Haiti has marked humanity with its prowess in 1804 when it put an end to slavery, racial discrimination, and colonization in St. Domingue, colony of France under the rule of Napoleon Bonaparte. This influenced the course of history in many parts of the world from France and the United States, to South America and all the other continents.

In this book, Jean Paul Jean François made the effort to compile the facts that should be known by all Haitians and those who are writing history about Haiti. This initiative debunks all the bad press that Haiti suffered because of its epic history.

Bito DaviD

CHAPTER I

Hayti/Haiti's Land – Population – Languages

❖ Haiti occupies the western third (27,750 km2, 10,710 sq mi) of the island of Hispaniola and the Dominican Republic the eastern two-thirds (48,445 km2, 18,705 sq mi) of the island. Approximately 700 miles southeast of Florida, the island is located between the island of Cuba, Jamaica and Puerto Rico. The name Hayti given by the Indians, first inhabitants of the island, means "mountainous land" in the Taino/Arawak Indian language; and "Haiti", the new spelling adopted in the 1930s, derives from Hayti.

❖ The population of Haiti was about 11 million in 2018. Most Haitians are of African descent with the rest of the population European, American and Middle-Eastern descents. The first African slaves arrived in Hayti in 1502.

HAITI: Contributions to the World

❖ The two national Languages of Haiti are French and Creole. The Haitian Creole Academy has existed since December 2014; however, French remains the language of Haiti's education curriculum.

French colony of Saint-Domingue in the West and Spanish colony of Santo Domingo in the East of Hispaniola Island during colonial years. The French side renamed Hayti after the Black slaves won their revolution on January 1, 1804.

HAITI: Contributions to the World

Hayti/Haiti, Pioneer of Freedom

In the late 18th century, Hayti contributed to free the world from more than two centuries of slavery through its successful and unprecedented slave revolt.

On August 14, 1791, Haytian slaves gathered at Morne Rouge (in the North of Haiti) in a congress followed by a religious ceremony called "Bwa Kay Man" under the direction of **Dutty Bookman and Cecile Fatima** to reject slavery as a crime against humanity. At the ceremony, the slaves vowed to fight slavery and planned a successful slave uprising the night of August 21st to 22nd 1791. **In reference to the Haytian revolution, August 23rd was chosen by the United Nations Educational, Scientific and Cultural Organization (UNESCO) as the International Day for the Remembrance of the Slave Trade and its Abolition.**

On November 7, 1791, **Bookman** was captured and hung by the French; **Toussaint Louverture** took over to lead the slaves until his capture and death in a dungeon at Fort de Joux in France on April 7, 1803.

On January 1st 1804, after the ultimate Battle of Vertières (Nov 18, 1803) under the leadership of **Jean-Jacques Dessalines**, Hayti became the first Independent nation of former Black slaves in the world and continued

HAITI: Contributions to the World

the fight to help and inspire the world to be free from slavery, segregation and colonization.

Frederic Douglass, a US diplomat in Hayti from 1889 to 1891, was inspired by the high price paid by the Haytian revolutionaries for the sake of freedom. He left a lasting appreciation of love and respect for Hayti in his poem "Until Hayti Spoke"

Frederick Douglass, 1889-1891 Minister and Consul-General to the Republic of Hayti.

"Until she spoke, no Christian nation had abolished Negro slavery.

Until she spoke, no Christian nation had given to the world an organized effort to abolish slavery.

Until she spoke, the slave ship, followed by hungry sharks, greedy to devour the dead and dying slaves flung overboard to feed them, ploughed in peace the South Atlantic, painting the sea with the Negro's blood.

Until she spoke, the slave trade was sanctioned by all the Christian nations of the world, and our land of liberty and light included.

Men made fortunes by this infernal traffic, and were esteemed as good Christians, and the standing types and representations of the Savior of the World.

Until Hayti spoke, the church was silent, and the pulpit was dumb.

Slave-traders lived and slave-traders died.

Funeral sermons were preached over them, and of them it was said that they died in the triumphs of the Christian faith and went to heaven among the just".

HAITI: Contributions to the World

A look at slavery before Hayti/Haiti Spoke

a) The Atlantic slave trade

From Wikipedia, the free encyclopedia

The **Atlantic slave trade** or **transatlantic slave trade** involved the transportation by slave traders of enslaved African people, mainly to the Americas. The slave trade regularly used the triangular trade route and its Middle Passage, and existed from the 16th to the 19th centuries. The vast majority of those who were enslaved and transported in the transatlantic slave trade were people from central and western Africa, who had been sold by other West Africans to Western European slave traders (with a small number being captured directly by the slave traders in coastal raids), who brought them to the Americas. The South Atlantic and Caribbean economies especially were dependent on the supply of secure labor for the production of commodity crops, making goods and clothing to sell in Europe. This was crucial to those western European countries, which, in the late 17th and 18th centuries, were vying with each other to create overseas empires.

HAITI: Contributions to the World

The Portuguese were the first to engage in the Atlantic slave trade in the 16th century. In 1526, they completed the first transatlantic slave voyage to Brazil, and other European countries soon followed. Ship owners regarded the slaves as cargo to be transported to the Americas as quickly and cheaply as possible, there to be sold to work on coffee, tobacco, cocoa, sugar and cotton plantations, gold and silver mines, rice fields, construction industry, cutting timber for ships, in skilled labor, and as domestic servants. The first Africans imported to the English colonies were classified as "indentured servants", like workers coming from England, and also as "apprentices for life". By the middle of the 17th century, slavery had hardened as a racial caste, with the slaves and their offspring being legally the property of their owners, and children born to slave mothers were also slaves. As property, the people were considered merchandise or units of labor, and were sold at markets with other goods and services.

The major Atlantic slave trading nations, ordered by trade volume were: the Portuguese, the British, the French, the Spanish, and the Dutch Empires. Several had established outposts on the African coast where they purchased slaves from local African leaders. These slaves were managed by a factor who was established on or near the coast to expedite the shipping of slaves to the New World. Slaves were kept in a factory while awaiting shipment. Current estimates are that about 12 million Africans were shipped across the Atlantic, although the number purchased by the traders was considerably higher, as the passage had a high death rate.

Near the beginning of the 19th century, various governments acted to ban the trade, although illegal smuggling still occurred. In the early 21st century, several governments issued apologies for the transatlantic slave trade.

HAITI: Contributions to the World

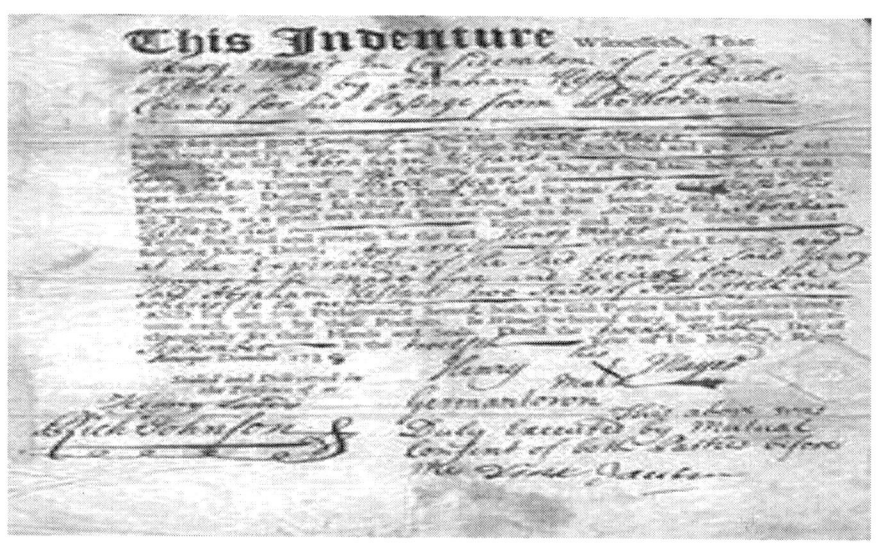

An indenture signed by Henry Mayer, with an "X", in 1738. This contract bound Mayer to Abraham Hestant of Bucks County, Pennsylvania, who had paid for Mayer to travel from Europe.

b) New World destinations

The first slaves to arrive as part of a labor force in the New World reached the island of Hispaniola (now Haiti and the Dominican Republic) in 1502. Cuba received its first four slaves in 1513. Jamaica received its first shipment of 4000 slaves in 1518. Slave exports to Honduras and Guatemala started in 1526.

The first enslaved Africans to reach what would become the United States arrived in July 1526 as part of a Spanish attempt to colonize San Miguel de Gualdape. By November, the 300 Spanish colonists were reduced to 100 and their slaves from 100 to 70. The enslaved people revolted in 1526 and joined a nearby Native American tribe, while the Spanish abandoned the colony altogether (1527). The area of the future Colombia received its first enslaved people in 1533. El Salvador, Costa Rica and Florida began their stints in the slave trade in 1541, 1563 and 1581, respectively.

The 17th century saw an increase in shipments. Africans arrived in the English colony of Jamestown, Virginia in 1619. The first kidnapped Africans in English North America were classed as indentured servants and freed after seven years. Virginia law codified chattel slavery in 1656, and in 1662, the colony adopted the principle of *partus sequitur ventrem*, which classified children of slave mothers as slaves, regardless of paternity. Irish immigrants took slaves to Montserrat in 1651, and in 1655, slaves were shipped to Belize.

Code Noir of 1742, Nantes history museum

The Code Noir (French pronunciation: [kɔd nwaʁ], Black Code) was a decree originally passed by France's King Louis XIV in 1685. The Code Noir defined the conditions of slavery in the French colonial empire, restricted the activities of free Negroes, forbade the exercise of any religion other than Roman Catholicism, and ordered all Jews out of France's colonies.

CHAPTER II

Hayti/Haiti's Contributions to the North American Countries:

The United States and Canada

A. Invaluable Contributions to the United States

1. The Battle of Savannah

Long before migrating to the United States in mass numbers, volunteer Haytian soldiers arrived to fight in one of the bloodiest battles of the American Revolution.

On October 9, 1779 a force of more than 500 Haytian troops known as the Chasseurs Volontaires de Saint-Domingue, appeared on the shores of Savannah, Ga. with a French fleet that helped save the Revolutionary army from slaughter by British troops. They were the largest unit of men of African descent to fight in the American Revolution. **One of its members was Henri Christophe who would later become President and king of Hayti (1807-1820). He built the Citadelle Laferrière**

(world heritage since 1982), the largest fortress in the Western Hemisphere.

After 228 years, the colored soldiers were finally recognized for their heroic actions. A monument to the Haytian soldiers was placed in Benjamin Franklin Square in Savannah, Georgia in 2007.

Statue of Haytian Soldiers at the Battle of Savannah, Franklin Square, Savannah, Georgia

HAITI: Contributions to the World

2. Haytian General Georges Biassou in St Augustine, Florida

Georges Biassou (1741, Hayti – 1801, Saint Augustine, Florida) was an early leader of the 1791 slave rising in Saint-Domingue that began the Haytian Revolution. With Jean François and Jeannot, he was prophesied by the vodou priest, Dutty Boukman, to lead the revolution.

Like some other slave leaders, he fought with the Spanish royalists against the French Revolutionary authorities in colonial Hayti. Defeated by his former ally Toussaint Louverture, who had allied with the French after they promised to free the slaves, Biassou remained in service to the Spanish Crown. He withdrew from Santo Domingo in 1795 and moved with his family to Florida, which was then part of the Spanish colony of Cuba.

In Florida, Biassou changed his first name to Jorge. Spanish leaders put him in charge of the black militia in Florida. He began to build alliances there when his brother-in-law married a fugitive from South Carolina. Florida had provided refuge for both planters and slaves during the American Revolution.

HAITI: Contributions to the World

3. The Purchase of Louisiana

The map of the United States had forever changed when Thomas Jefferson was able to acquire the Louisiana Territory from Napoleon because the French general was unable to subdue Haytian troops trained by **Toussaint Louverture and Jean Jacques Dessalines**.

The Louisiana Purchase of 1803 due to the failure of France to put down a slave revolution in Hayti, has brought into the United States about 828,000,000 square miles of territory from France, thereby doubling the size of the young republic. What was known at the time as the Louisiana Territory stretched from the Mississippi River in the east to the Rocky Mountains in the west and from the Gulf of Mexico in the south to the Canadian border in the north. Part or all of 15 states were eventually created from the land deal, which is considered one of the most important achievements of Thomas Jefferson's presidency.

HAITI: Contributions to the World

4. Hayti inspired slave revolt in the U.S.

In 1800, as events continued to unfold in Hayti; slave rebellions were taking place in Virginia under the leadership of **Gabriel Prosser** and in Charleston, South Carolina with **Denmark Vesey**. The exploits of **Toussaint Louverture** and **Jean Jacques Dessalines** in Hayti were a particular inspiration to both leaders.

On August 30, 1800, **Gabriel Prosser** assembled 1000 slaves outside Richmond to capture the state capital of Virginia. A heavy rain that washed out bridges and roads limited **Prosse**r and his cohorts in executing their insurrection. Making things worse, an informer already alerted authorities about the revolt.

As a result, the Virginia authorities easily captured many of the assembled slaves. **Prosser** managed to escape, but was eventually captured on board a ship in Norfolk. He was taken to Richmond and summarily hanged.

In 1822, the murmur of freedom and equality circulating among Charleston's population turned to action, as **Denmark Vesey** hatched a plot for a slave uprising. More than 9,000 slaves and free blacks were attracted to Vesey's plot to free the city of Charleston.

Before the revolt could fully hold, however, several slaves betrayed the conspirators, forcing **Vesey** into hiding and leading to the arrest of 130 of his co-conspirators. Ultimately, **Vesey** was found by local authorities and quickly hung, as were many other rebels. Charleston's aborted rebellion would have been the largest slave uprising in U.S history.

In the investigation and hearing that followed the rebellion's discovery, it was found that **Denmark Vesey** and his co-conspirators had been in touch with President Jean-Pierre Boyer of Hayti. Indeed, one of **Vesey**'s lieutenants, Monday Gell, had written two letters to the president of Hayti seeking support for the planned insurrection.

5. President Boyer of Hayti welcomed African-Americans in 1820

Throughout his political career, Jean-Pierre Boyer always expressed interest in the African-Americans who were still living in slavery and segregation in the United States. Once became president, Boyer invited the African-Americans to immigrate to Hayti in a formal invitation letter. The government of Jean-Pierre Boyer implemented a policy **called the Society for Promoting the Emigration of Free Persons of Color to Hayti.** In addition, the government offered incentive such as free trips, 10 pounds of coffee, three acres of land and money per family upon their arrival in Hayti.

As a result of Boyer's immigration policy and his emissary Jonathan Granville, several thousands of African-Americans went to settle in Hayti. One of the first African-Americans to hear the call of Hayti was Henri Simonise, a mulatto born in South Carolina, and educated in England. Simonise emigrated to Hayti in 1818 to escape the humiliation of daily life in the United States. Here is the reproduction of Boyer's invitation letter by **Nile's Weekly Register.**

NILES' WEEKLY REGISTER.

HAYTI.

"President Boyer is inviting the free blacks of the United States to emigrate to Hayti, in preference to Africa, promising them protection and assistance. An address to the Haytians on this subject says—"Our past sufferings—our unexampled efforts to regain our primitive rights—our solemn oath to live free and independent—the happy situation of our island, which may be justly called the queen of the Antilles—the astonishing fertility of its soil, which makes it the garden of the western archipelago—the progress of its inhabitants in civilization, and in some of the fine arts; our wise constitution which insures a free country to Africans and their descendants; all lead us to believe that the hand of Providence has destined Hayti for a land of promise, a sacred asylum, where our unfortunate brethren will, in the end, see their wounds healed by the balm of equality, and their tears wiped away by the protecting hand of liberty."

6. Haytian Emperor Faustin Soulouque and President Fabre Nicolas Geffrard Immigration Policies toward African-Americans

Following the previous policy of Jean-Pierre Boyer to welcome African-Americans in Hayti, new efforts were launched by Emperor Faustin Soulouque in 1855 and the government of Fabre Nicolas Geffrard in 1859 on the settling of African Americans in the island of Hayti. Geffrard appointed James Redpath to attract immigrants to the island; he encouraged the immigration of African-Americans, especially Catholic farmers from Louisiana. Between 1859 and 1860 an estimated 500 blacks from Louisiana immigrated to Hayti. In May 1861, led by a Black Episcopal priest, James Theodore Holly, a group of African-Americans numbering nearly 2000 emigrated from New Haven, Connecticut to Hayti.

The Franco-African Peoples of Haiti and Louisiana Population, Language, Culture, Religion, and Revolution

By Gwendolyn Midlo Hall

There are important similarities and differences between the creative, vibrant, and indomitable peoples

HAITI: Contributions to the World

who created the cultures of Saint-Domingue/Haiti and Louisiana. Both places were colonized by France. Some of the colonizers of both places were pirates. Although Saint-Domingue/Haiti remained a French colony until it achieved its independence in 1804, Spain took effective control of Louisiana by 1770 and the United States by 1804. Despite these changes in administration, Louisiana's population remained almost entirely French, Cajun and Creole speakers. The languages survived widely in rural areas until the mid-twentieth century and are still spoken today in some places in southwest Louisiana.

The colonizing population of Saint-Domingue/Haiti and Louisiana was both similar and different. Saint-Domingue's Native American population, the Arawak, had developed an extraordinarily just, productive, spiritual, and artistic civilization. The first Africans were introduced in 1502 by the Spanish. During the first few decades of Spanish colonization, the Arawak and enslaved Africans, first Ladinos who were African-born or socialized in Spain, and then mainly Africans of the Wolof ethnicity brought directly from Senegal, cooperated in revolts against the Spanish rule. The Ladinos and then the Wolof taught the Arawak how to revolt effectively against the Spanish and the Arawak helped the Africans escape to the mountains and create runaway slave communities.

But before French rule began in Saint-Domingue/Haiti, the Arawak population had been utterly destroyed as corporate groups by the Spanish conquerors and colonizers.

In sharp contrast, in Louisiana, the first slaves were Native Americans. Several of these nations, including Alabama, Attakapas, Choctaw, Chickasaw, Creek, Mobile, Natchez, Natchitoches, and Tunica remained powerful throughout the eighteen century. While some colonizers of Louisiana were born in France, many were Canadian coureurs de bois who lived among and merged with Native Americans both biologically and culturally. Africans often allied and merged with Native Americans as well. Following the same patterns as in early Saint-Domingue/Haiti, Africans taught Native Americans how to combat Spanish and French methods of warfare, and Native Americans helped Africans escape to the forests and swamps and create runaway slave communities. (Whites with deep roots in Louisiana often have ancestors who were African slaves as well as Native Americans, but they were rarely acknowledged after a few generations, especially the Africans.) Thus, Louisiana was a frontier society where peoples of various racial designations and cultures mingled freely. In contrast, in Saint- Domingue, the vast majority of the population were enslaved Africans and their descendants, slave and free, black and mixed blood. Both Haiti and Louisiana had a very competent, wealthy mulatto or mixed blood free Creole elite.

Both Saint-Domingue/Haiti and Louisiana had slave systems, but large scale commercial agriculture geared toward the export of crops developed much earlier in Saint-Domingue/Haiti than in Louisiana. Two distinctive Franco-African Creole languages were created in Haiti and in Louisiana. Louisiana Creole developed within the first decade of the arrival of the first transatlantic slave trade ships in 1719. Two-thirds of these Africans were brought from Senegambia. As a result, the Louisiana Creole language is closest to the Creole of Mauritius Island in the Indian Ocean, where Senegambians were also the formative African population. Folktales and proverbs in Louisiana Creole, most notably the Bouki/Lapin stories, are mainly Wolof in origin. But terms for religious amulets, for example gris-gris and zinzin derive from Mande languages, which were the lingua franca in Senegambia throughout the Atlantic slave trade.

HAITI: Contributions to the World

Both Haiti and Louisiana were deeply influenced by massive imports of Africans, but their ethnic origins and the timing of their arrival varied.

Senegambians were feared in the Caribbean because of their rebelliousness. But they were preferred in colonies which became part of the United States, especially Louisiana and South Carolina, where rice and indigo were widely cultivated and slaves were barely a majority and therefore less feared. It was a matter of technology transfer from Africa to America. Africans taught Europeans how to cultivate and process rice and indigo crops, which had been domesticated and produced in Greater Senegambia for many centuries before the transatlantic slave trade, began.

The religious influence of Africans living near the coasts of the Bight of Benin, especially the Dahomeans, was strong in both Saint-Domingue/Haiti and Louisiana. These Gbe language-group speakers were usually recorded as Arada in documents in Saint-Domingue and as Fon(d), Aja, Arada, or Mina in Louisiana, but sometimes in Saint-Domingue as well. The vodou gods of both Haiti and Louisiana derived from Dahomean gods. There were six recorded transatlantic slave trade voyages from the Bight of Benin that arrived to French Louisiana, the last in 1728. Africans from this coast came to be *prized in the parishes upriver from New Orleans and were sought out by Louisiana slave owners during the transshipment trade to Louisiana from the Caribbean Islands. Slaves from the Bight of Benin were brought directly from Africa to Saint-Domingue in large numbers before 1750. After 1750, the transatlantic slave trade to Saint-Domingue tilted heavily toward West Central Africa. Almost all West Central Africans were listed as Congo and they were clustered in coffee-growing regions. The Congo began to arrive in Louisiana in large numbers much later, after 1780. They were concentrated in and near New Orleans, especially after sugar became a major crop in Louisiana.*

There is little evidence that significant numbers of Saint-Domingue/Haiti slaves or free people of color were brought to Louisiana during the eighteenth century. Export of slaves from the French Caribbean islands was first discouraged and then outlawed in 1763, because they were considered dangerous poisoners; no doubt, a reaction to the Makandal conspiracy of 1758 aimed at abolishing slavery. After the great slave revolt erupted in Saint-Domingue/Haiti in 1971, serious efforts were made to keep slaves from this colony out of Louisiana. These included outlawing the foreign slave trade and at times allowing only new Africans to be brought in.

HAITI: Contributions to the World

No doubt, some slaves from Saint-Domingue were brought in illegally. But there is no evidence in the extensive surviving testimony of slaves involved in conspiracies and revolts against slavery that any slaves or free people of color from Saint-Domingue participated in any of them. The resistance of Louisiana slaves to slavery, while inspired at times by the Haitian revolution, was never led by Haitians. During the Age of Revolutions, they were led almost entirely by Louisiana Creole slaves, along with some enslaved Africans brought to Louisiana directly from Africa.

The long, bloody slave revolution of Haiti produced many refugees. They went in waves to various places in the Americas. The main contingent of these refugees to Louisiana arrived very late. During 1809 and 1810, shiploads of refugees from the Haitian Revolution entered the port of New Orleans. They totaled about 10,000 people. About one-third of them were white elite, another one-third free-colored elite, and the other one-third slaves were property of either elite group. A special law was passed by the congress of the United States allowing these refugees and their slaves to enter Louisiana because their slaves were considered very loyal to their masters and not a danger to Louisiana's slave system.

HAITI: Contributions to the World

Who were the Haitians refugees? The free colored elite left Saint-Domingue after they had been defeated by the slaves revolting against slavery led by Toussaint Louverture and Jean-Jacques Dessalines. Almost all of them had gone to nearby Santiago on the extreme eastern end of the island of Cuba before Haitian independence triumphed. These refugees brought the coffee industry to Cuba and were very knowledgeable about sugar production. Although they had made a great contribution to the Cuban economy, they were expelled from Cuba after France invaded Spain in 1809 and anti-French sentiment boiled over. Louisiana was especially attractive to them because the Louisiana Creole language had been created by African slaves who arrived in Louisiana almost a century earlier. Louisiana Creole is close enough to Haitian Creole that speakers of these two languages could understand each other. French was the language of the elites of both Haiti and Louisiana, although they were also speakers of the Creole languages. The climate was warm, humid, and familiar. Both Saint-Domingue and Louisiana had prosperous slave plantation systems growing some of the same crops: sugar, cotton, and indigo. When the Haitian refugees expelled from Santiago de Cuba arrived in Louisiana during 1809 and 1810, their slaves remained almost entirely in New Orleans. They were mostly young, female domestics.

There was much unrest among Louisiana slaves, even before the slave revolt in Haiti. In July 1791, a month before the slaves revolted in Haiti, there was a conspiracy among Mina slaves in Pointe Coupée Parish, Louisiana, to rise up and abolish slavery. Throughout the Haitian Revolution, there were conspiracies against slavery as well as mass runaways among Louisiana slaves. Louisiana slaves were very well aware that the slaves in Saint-Domingue/Haiti were fighting against their masters to abolish slavery. The 1795 slave conspiracy in Pointe Coupée was inspired by the slave revolt in Haiti as well as by the slaves' knowledge that the French National Assembly had abolished slavery in French colonies in 1794. **Joseph Bouavel**, a Walloon (Franco-Belgian) teacher-tailor in Pointe Coupée, read to the slaves from the Declaration of the Rights of Man.

In 1811, the biggest revolt in the history of slavery in the United States took place on the German Coast in the parishes along the Mississippi River north of New Orleans. Historians have long tried to portray Louisiana slaves as incompetent, content and passive, attributing all unrest among them to "outside influences". Charles Gayarrée, a white Creole historian of the nineteenth century, claimed *that Charles Deslondes, the main leader of the 1811 Revolt, was a free man of color from Haiti. But he was actually a mulatto Louisiana Creole slave. On October 15, 1795, he was listed as a Creole mulatto, age 18, inventoried among the slaves of his deceased master Deslondes. He was listed as a slave of the widow of Jacques Deslondes in a document dated January 13, 1811, which listed slaves involved in this revolt. There was a free man of color named Charles involved in the 1811 revolt who was a mulatto, but he too was a Louisiana Creole.*

Nevertheless, misinformation about Charles Deslondes' status and origin has been passed down through the generations, misidentifying him as a free man of color from Haiti. This is an example of racist historiography, which assumes that Louisiana slaves were happy with slavery and/or too incompetent to resist without "outside agitators" to instigate and lead them. **While the antislavery movements among Louisiana slaves during the Age of Revolutions were** *partially inspired by the success of the Haitian Revolution and the instability of the times, there is no evidence of direct involvement by Haitians in any Louisiana conspiracies and revolts against slavery.*

HAITI: Contributions to the World

The presence of Haitian refugees in Louisiana doubled the free colored population of New Orleans. They certainly influenced Louisiana's evolving Creole culture, especially among Louisiana's mixed blood elite. There was intermarriage between members of the Louisiana and Haitian free colored elite refugees. Many of their descendants trace at least some of their ancestors to Haiti. But the cultural influence of these Haitian refugees in Louisiana has been exaggerated. They arrived long after the Louisiana Creole language, folklore, cuisine, and music had been created by enslaved peoples brought directly to Louisiana from Africa and by their Louisiana Creole descendants. Many of the slaves brought in by these Haitian refugees were born in Cuba, not in Haiti. Many of them were young, with little or no memory of Haiti. As mentioned, the slaves brought in by Haitian refugees remained almost entirely in New Orleans. Their direct impact on unrest among Louisiana slaves was not likely to be great, especially in rural areas. The unrest among Louisiana slaves during the Age of Revolutions stemmed mainly from their competence, their courage, and their love of freedom.

The Haitian Revolution was an extraordinary achievement. It was the only successful slave revolt in the Western Hemisphere. It was the second successful independence movement in the Western Hemisphere. After achieving its own independence, Haiti helped and inspired the Latin American independence wars that began in 1810. President Pétion of Haiti gave refuge and support to Simon Bolivar and his followers after their movement suffered reverses in South America, in exchange for Bolivar's promise to abolish slavery when Latin America became independent. The entire world owes much to the Haitian Revolution. It is one of very few instances of the triumph of a movement for freedom among slaves anywhere at any time. It was a vanguard of independence throughout the Americas. Our debt to Haiti, the Haitian Revolution, and the Haitian people has not yet been recognized.

HAITI: Contributions to the World

7. Contributions of Haytian Immigrants to the U.S from 1700s to Present

Haytian immigrants have started to enrich the U.S soil in the late 1700s. **Jean Baptiste Point du Sable**, born in St Marc, was the founder of Chicago by establishing the first permanent dwelling near the Chicago River.

Pierre Toussaint established one of the first children orphanage in the United States in 1811; Toussaint is the only Haitian American recognized for canonization by the Catholic Church, he received from Pope John Paul II the title of Venerable in 1996.

Mother Elizabeth Lange who founded Saint Francis Academy in 1828, the oldest Black school in the United States are examples of Haytian-born slaves who have contributed to build the American society.

The most recent examples of Haitian contributions to the American culture come from thousands of immigrants from Haiti to the United States. In the late 1950's a significant group of educated Haitians fled the oppression of the Duvalier regime and assimilated into the social fabric of New York City, particularly Brooklyn, Spring Valley and later Miami. Among those Haitians who have served as soldiers, educators, judges, legislators, advisors to the legislative branch of US government, private service industries are:

Dr. Rose-Marie Toussaint, physician, first black female served as chief surgeon for the liver transplant center at Howard University Hospital.

Pierre-Richard Prosper, Ambassador-at-Large, Office of War Crime Issues nominated by President Georges W. Bush.

Marie P. St. Fleur, first Haitian-born individual elected to state office in the United States.

Marie Ferdinand-Harris, first Haitian-American to play in the WNBA.

Gerald A. Alphonse, Haitian electrical engineer, physicist and research scientist, president of the United States division of the Institute of Electrical and Electronic Engineers in 2005.

André Birotte Jr., former United States Attorney was sworn in on August 8, 2014 as a federal district judge for the United States District Court, Central District of California.

Judge Birotte was nominated by President Barack Obama on April 3, 2014. He was confirmed unanimously

HAITI: Contributions to the World

by the Senate on July 22, 2014, **Birotte** was born in Newark, New Jersey, in 1966 to Haitian immigrants.

Kwame Raoul, first Haitian-American Senator, Chicago, Illinois is the son of Haitian-born immigrants. On November 6, 2004, he was chosen by Democratic committee members to replace Barack Obama in the Illinois Senate. He became the 42nd Attorney General of Illinois in 2019.

Judge Fred Seraphin, first Haitian-American judge of South Florida.

Linda Dorcena Forry, first Haitian-American elected in Massachusetts State Senate (May 2013).

Ludmya "Mia" Bourdeau Love, Haitian-American, first black female Republican elected to the U.S Congress, serving from 2015 to 2019.

Daphnee Campbell, first Haitian-American elected to the Florida State Senate (November 2016).

Karl A. Racine, Haitian-born American lawyer and politician was elected Attorney-General of the District of Columbia since 2015.

Edwidge Danticat, Haitian-American professor, writer, novelist. She is the author of numerous books including

"Brother, I'm Dyying" which won the National Book Critics Circle Award.

Phillip J. Brutus, first Haitian elected to the Florida House of Representative in 2000; he was also the first city Councilman. He co-sponsored a bill adopted on April 22, 2004 to recognize January 1, 2004 "Republic of Haiti Day" and the Haitian heroes as world heroes for their contributions to the world. As a result, in the city of North Miami, several streets are named after the Haitian heroes Toussaint Louverture, Jean-Jacques Dessalines, Capois Lamort, Henri Christophe and Alexandre Petion.

8. May is Haitian Heritage Month in the United States

Haitian Heritage Month is a celebration in the United States of Haitian heritage and culture. It was first celebrated in Boston, Massachusetts, in 1998.

The Haitian community in the state of Florida contributed greatly to make the Heritage Month first a statewide celebration, and then, a national one in the United States. South Florida congressman **Kendrick B. Meek** introduced unsuccessfully a bill in the United States House of Representatives in 2003 and 2006 to recognize the month of May as Haitian-American Heritage Month in the United States. President **George W. Bush** and his wife **Laura Bush** sent a letter on April 2006 to congratulate the Haitian-American community for the heritage month and organized a celebration at the White House the same year.

Since 1998, several governors, members of state senates and houses of representatives, mayors and city councilors have issued annual citations and proclamations, recognizing the Haitian Heritage celebration in their states or cities.

HAITI: Contributions to the World

THE WHITE HOUSE

WASHINGTON

April 28, 2006

I send greetings to those celebrating Haitian American Heritage Month.

Our Nation is more dynamic thanks to the traditions and contributions of citizens of many different backgrounds. Haitian Americans have helped shape our national character and strengthen our country. This month is an opportunity to celebrate Haitian ancestry and highlight your proud history and rich culture.

I applaud Haitian Americans for preserving and sharing your heritage. Your efforts add vitality to our country and enhance the diversity that makes America strong.

Laura and I send our best wishes.

HAITI: Contributions to the World

RESOLUTION

HAITIAN HERITAGE MONTH

WHEREAS, the growth and prosperity of Palm Beach County, Florida, is due in part to an ethnic diversity that includes a substantial and rapidly increasing Haitian population; and

WHEREAS, we recognize the valuable contributions of the Haitian people in the fight for the independence of the United States of America, especially in the battle of Savannah, and pay due tribute to their endowment; and

WHEREAS, the Haitian population in South Florida joins together during the month of May to commemorate their "Flag Day" and celebrate their historical and cultural identity; and

WHEREAS, it is appropriate to promote awareness, and understanding of cultural diversity in our society in order to strengthen the self-esteem of our multicultural student population and improve their academic achievement;

NOW, THEREFORE, BE IT RESOLVED that the Superintendent and the School Board of Palm Beach County School District do hereby recognize the month of May as Haitian Heritage Month and showcase the unique diversity of the Haitian culture and contributions.

Done this twenty-third day of April 2003, in West Palm Beach, Florida.

Arthur C. Johnson, Ph.D., Superintendent   Mr. Tom Lynch, Chair

B. Hayti/Haiti's Contributions to Canada

Canada's relations with Hayti date back to the early 18th century. There are records of immigration from Hayti to Quebec dating from the 1700s, when both were part of the French Empire. Exchange slowed as France lost its colonies in the New World in the late18th century.

Relations between Canada and Haiti grew again in the early 20th century, this time between French-speaking elites in both countries. French Canadians began to replace the French and Belgian missionaries, dispersed by the World Wars, who had dominated Haiti's Catholic community.

Meanwhile the educated Haitian elite chose Quebec as a destination for education and immigration. These French-speaking immigrants integrated well into Canadian society. In 1964, **Dr. Saint-Firmin Monestime**, who had moved to the francophone community of Mattawa, Ontario, was elected as the first black mayor in Canada and remained mayor until his death in 1977. **Monestime** is fondly remembered for his contribution to the early history of the city of Mattawa. There is an exhibit at the Mattawa Museum in his honor.

Dany Laferrière, born Windson Kléber Laferrière in Haiti, novelist, essayist, poet, and journalist. Winner of the prestigious Prix Medicis and the first Haitian-Canadian to be elected to the Académie Française. Laferrière is the second black person to have been inducted in 2013; the first was a Senegalese writer and statesman, Léopold Sédar Senghor in 1983. Dany Laferrière has established himself as one of the premiere chroniclers of the immigrant experience and one of the finest novelists of his generation.

On June 3, 2014, he was awarded the International Literature Award by the House of World Cultures for his novel *The Return* (*L'enigme du retour*).

In 2014, he was appointed officer of the National Order of Quebec.

In 2015, **Laferrière** was awarded the Order of Canada with the grade of officer.

In 2016, **Laferrière** won the Martin Luther King Jr. Achievement Award for his literary achievements.

HAITI: Contributions to the World

The most invaluable contribution of Haitian immigrants to Canada is Her Excellency the Right Honorable **Michaëlle Jean**, Governor General of Canada from 2005 to 2010.

Michaëlle Jean, (born September 6, 1957, Port-au-Prince, Haiti), Canadian journalist and documentarian who was Canada's 27th governor-general (2005–10) and the first person of African heritage to hold that post.

Michaëlle Jean parents are Haitian Immigrants. Her father suffered imprisonment and torture under the regime of François Duvalier, leading to the family's flight to Canada when she was 11. They settled in Montreal. Jean proved to be a brilliant student, studying languages and literature at the University of Montreal, where she earned a master's degree in comparative literature. She also attended universities in Italy and France.

Sworn in on 27 September 2005, she succeeded Adrienne Clarkson. **Jean** became the first black person to serve as governor general. The descendant of slaves, she used her office to passionately emphasize freedom as a central part of the Canadian identity. Reflecting on her experience as an immigrant, **Jean** argued that it was time to "eliminate the spectra" of the two solitudes, French and English, which had long characterized the country's history.

As governor general, **Jean** showed herself to be a passionate speaker and a photogenic presence. She used her office to advance human rights, support the arts, draw attention to socio-economic problems in the Canadian north, and promote Canada abroad, particularly in Africa and her native Haiti.

On October 1, 2010, Jean was replaced as governor general by David Johnston. She became UNESCO's special envoy to Haiti and created the Michaëlle Jean Foundation to help underprivileged youth in rural and northern Canada.

On 30 November 2014, she was appointed Secretary-General of the Organization Internationale de La Francophonie (International Organization of La Francophonie) during the 15th summit of French-speaking nation in Dakar, Senegal. She is the first woman and the first Haitian-Canadian to hold that position.

CHAPTER III

Hayti/Haiti's Contributions to the Dominican Republic

In 1818, Jean-Pierre Boyer succeeded Alexandre Pétion as President of Hayti. Two years later, upon the death of King Henri Christophe, Boyer brought the Northen Province under his jurisdiction, reuniting the North, West and South of Hayti. In February 1822, Boyer expended the national territory significantly in unifying the west part the island (Hayti) to the east (Dominican Republic) which was known as **Republic of Spanish Hayti** after its independence from Spain on Dec 1, 1821.

Dominican Republic: Independence from Spain

On November 9, 1821, the Spanish colony of Santo Domingo was toppled by a group led by José Núñez de Cáceres, the colony's former administrator, and the rebels proclaimed independence from the Spanish crown on December 1, 1821. The new nation was known as **Republic of Spanish Hayti** (Spanish: *República del Haytí Español*), as *Hayti* had been the indigenous name of the island. On the day of December 1, 1821, a constitutive act was ordered to petition the union of **Spanish Hayti** with Gran Colombia.

Prelude to the Unification of West (Hayti) to East (Spanish Hayti)

To secure its independence, a group of Dominican politicians and military officers favored uniting the newly independent nation with Hayti, as they sought for political stability under Haytian president Jean-Pierre Boyer, and were attracted to Hayti's perceived wealth and power at the time. A large faction based in the northern Cibao region was opposed to the union with Gran Colombia and also sided with Hayti. Boyer, on the other hand, had several objectives in the island that he proclaimed to be "one and indivisible": to maintain Haytian independence against potential French or Spanish attack and to maintain the freedom of its former slaves.

While appeasing the Dominican officers, Jean-Pierre Boyer was already in negotiations with France to prevent an attack by fourteen French warships stationed near Port-au-Prince, the Haytian capital. The Dominicans were unaware that Boyer made a concession to the French, and agreed to pay France 150 million gold francs destined to compensate the former French slave owners. Thus, Hayti would essentially be forced into paying reparations for its freedom.

The Dominican nationalists who were against the unification of the island were at a serious disadvantage if they were to maintain their nation's sovereignty. At the time, they had an untrained infantry force. The population was eight to ten times less than Hayti's, and the economy was stalled. Hayti, on the other hand, had formidable armed forces, both in skill and sheer size, which had been hardened in nearly ten years of repelling French Napoleon soldiers, and British soldiers, along with the local colonialists and military insurgents within the country. The racial massacres perpetrated in the later days of the French–Haytian conflict only added to the determination of Haytians to never lose a battle.

Support of the unification found itself to be more popular amongst the mixed race and Black populations who believed that Boyer's government would usher an era of social reform and the subsequent abolition of slavery. In contrast, the Creole population, however, found itself split on the idea of merging with the neighboring country. After deals with Bolivar fell through and receiving messages of economic and military support from Boyer, Caceres found himself more obliged to side with Creole Hayti. The idea had been gaining some traction among members of the military, and in 1821, Governor Sebastián Kindelán discovered that some of the Dominican military officers in Azua and Santo Domingo had already become part of the plan for unification with Hayti.

A defining moment took place on November 15, 1821, when the leaders of several Dominican border towns, particularly Dajabón and Montecristi, adopted the Haytian flag.

Unification

After promising his full support to several Dominican governors and securing their allegiance, Boyer ceremoniously entered the country with around 10,000 soldiers in February 1822, encountering little to no opposition. On February 9, 1822, Boyer formally entered the capital city, Santo Domingo after its ephemeral independence, where he was met with enthusiasm and received by Núñez de Cáceres who offered to him the keys of the Palace; Boyer rejected the offer saying: *"I have not come into this city as a conqueror but by the will of its inhabitants"*. The island was thus united from Cape Tiburon to Cape Samana in possession of one government.

HAITI: Contributions to the World

Resistance

In 1838 a group of educated nationalists, among them, Juan Pablo Duarte, Matías Ramón Mella, and Francisco del Rosario Sánchez founded a secret society called *La Trinitaria* to gain independence from Hayti. In 1843, they allied with a Haytian movement that overthrew Boyer in Hayti. After they revealed themselves as revolutionaries working for Dominican independence, the new Haytian president, Charles Rivière-Hérard, exiled or imprisoned the leading *Trinitarios*. At the same time, Buenaventura Báez, an Azua mahogany exporter and deputy in the Haytian National Assembly, was negotiating with the French Consul-General for the establishment of a French protectorate.

In an uprising timed to preempt Báez, on February 27, 1844, the Trinitarios declared independence from Hayti, backed by Pedro Santana, a wealthy cattle-rancher from El Seibo who commanded a private army of peons who worked on his estates. This marked the beginning of the Dominican War of Independence.

CHAPTER IV

Hayti/Haiti's contributions to the South and Central American Countries

Hayti contributed more to the liberation of the South Americans from European colonial powers than any other nation. Several countries in Latin America have obtained their independence with the help of Hayti.

In 1804, the commander of Jacmel, Magloire Ambroise was one of the generals who signed the independence act. In February 1806, by the order of Dessalines, Magloire Ambroise received Francisco de Miranda (a South American leader who fought to liberate Latin America from Spanish rule) and gave Miranda munitions and men to fight the Spaniards. The following month, March 12, 1806, the Venezuelan flag was born in the harbor of Jacmel. In Venezuela, this day is celebrated as flag's day.

In 1806, **Alexandre Pétion**, one of the Haytian heroes who fought alongside **Jean-Jacques Dessalines** for the

HAITI: Contributions to the World

independence of Hayti became the president of Hayti after the assassination of **Dessalines** on October 17, 1806. Under the leadership of Alexandre Pétion, Hayti provided military assistance including money, weapons, ammunitions and volunteer soldiers to the Spanish revolutionist Simon Bolivar to help free what is known today as the Bolivarian countries in South and Central America.

Twice Hayti, through President Pétion, helped Simon Bolivar who arrived in Haiti in December 1815 downtrodden and accompanied by Venezuelan families and soldiers after being badly trampled by the Spanish in Cartagena, Bolivia as he attempted to free South American countries, which are now Venezuela, Colombia, Peru, Chile, and Bolivia. Upon his arrival in Les Cayes, Hayti, Bolivar was desperate and sought refuge and help to conquer the Spanish Army. President Alexandre Pétion agreed to help Bolivar and his associates. The only condition he demanded that he freed the slaves in all the countries that became independent. They stayed in Les Cayes long enough to heal and regroup. During their stay (3 months), President Pétion gave them shelter and food. When they were leaving, President Pétion gave them 4,000 rifles, gunpowder, cartridges, food and a printing press.

HAITI: Contributions to the World

Bolivar returned to Hayti after six months admitting that he made tactical errors; as a result, he was separated from the main body of his army. President Pétion again helped Bolivar and when they were leaving the island in December 1816, the President gave him not only supplies but also 300 Haytian soldiers. Bolivar's fight was not easy, it was rather very difficult, but ultimately he successfully obtained the independence of modern-day north-west Brazil, Guyana, Venezuela, Ecuador, Colombia, Panama, northern Peru, Costa Rica, Nicaragua, and Bolivia. As promised to Pétion, Simon Bolivar abolished slavery in those territories.

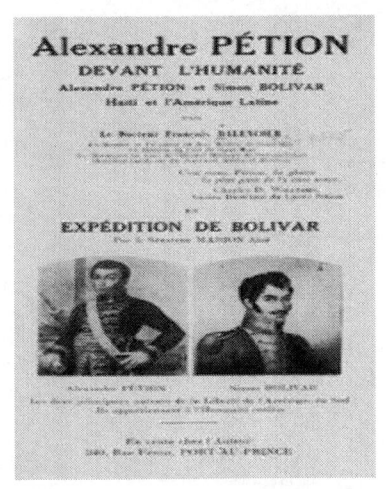

Pétion and Bolívar, Haiti and Latin America (1929) by François Dalencour. From the University of Florida George A. Smathers Library.

CHAPTER V

Hayti/Haiti's contributions to the European, African and Middle-Eastern countries

A. Contributions to Greece

Hayti, famous for its open-arms policy to all territories fighting for self-determination, was the first government of an independent state that recognized the Greek revolution against the Turkish Empire. Jean-Pierre Boyer, following a Greek request for assistance, addressed a letter on January 15, 1822. In the letter sent to Greek expatriates living in France, Adamantios Korais, Christodoulos Klonaris, Christodoulos Klonaris, Konstantinos Polychroniades and A. Bogorides, who had assembled themselves into a Committee which was seeking international support for the ongoing Greek revolution, expressed his support for the Greek Revolution and compared the struggle underfoot across the Atlantic to the struggle for independence in his own land. Boyer apologized for being unable to support the Revolution in Greece financially, though he hoped he might be able to in the future. But he articulated his moral and political support for the revolution, notably by filling his letter with references to classical Greek history, demonstrating a detailed knowledge of this history and powerfully evoking the contemporary revolutionaries as the rightful heirs of their ancestors.

Some historians claim that Boyer also sent to the Greeks 25 tons of Haytian coffee that could be sold and the proceeds used to purchase weapons, but not enough evidence exists to support this or the other claim that one hundred Haytian volunteers set off to fight in the Greek Revolution. Allegedly, their ship was boarded by pirates somewhere in the Mediterranean and these fighters reportedly never reached their destination.

Here is the letter to the Greeks:

JEAN-PIERRE BOYER

President of Hayti

To the citizens of Greece A. Korais, K. Polychoroniades, A. Bogorides and Ch. Klonaris.

In Paris

"Before I received your letter from Paris, dated last August 20, the news about the revolution of your co-citizens against the despotism which lasted for about three centuries had already arrived here. With great enthusiasm we learned that Hellas was finally forced to take up arms in order to gain her freedom and the position that she once held among the nations of the world. Such a beautiful and just case, most importantly, the first successes, which have accompanied it, cannot leave Haytians indifferent, for we, like the Hellenes, were for a long time subjected to a dishonorable slavery and finally, with our own chains, broke the head of tyranny.

Wishing to Heavens to protect the descendants of Leonidas, we thought to assist these brave warriors, if not with military forces and ammunition, at least with money, which will be useful for acquisition of guns, which you need. But events that have occurred and imposed financial restrictions onto our country absorbed the entire budget, including the part that could be disposed by our administration. Moreover, at present, the revolution, which triumphs on the eastern portion of our island, is creating a new obstacle in carrying out our aim; in fact, this portion, which was incorporated into the Republic I preside over, is in extreme poverty and thus justifies immense expenditures of our budget. If the circumstances, as we wish, improve again, then we shall honorably assist you, the sons of Hellas, to the best of our abilities.

Citizens! Convey to your co-patriots the warm wishes that the people of Hayti send on the behalf of your liberation. The descendants of ancient Hellenes look forward, in the reawakening of their history, to trophies worthy of Salamis. May they prove to be like their ancestors and guided by the commands of Miltiades, and be able, in the fields of new Marathon, to achieve the triumph of the holy affair that they have undertaken on behalf of their rights, religion and motherland. May it be, at last, through their wise decisions, that they will be commemorated by history as the heirs of the endurance and virtues of their ancestors.

In the 15th of January 1822 and the 19th year of Independence"

BOYER

B. Contributions to Libya, Somalia and Israel

Haiti has contributed to the independence of Libya, Israel and Somalia through its ambassador to the United Nations, **Emile Saint-Lot.**

Emile Saint-Lot served as the first ambassador of Haiti to the United Nations in 1945, and a member of the Security Council responsible for voting on the independence of countries. He was decisive for the independence of **Somalia, Israel, and Libya**. As for the latter, he was convinced by Ali Aneizi, member of the Liberation of Libya committee, to vote against the Bevin-Sforza Plan, a plan to make the three regions of Libya (Tripolitania, Cyrenaica, Fezzan) under the trusteeship of three countries (Italy, United Kingdom, France, respectively). The necessary votes to adopt the plan were never attained as a result of **Saint-Lot** voting against it.

Emile Saint-Lot senator of Haiti in 1946 was a delegate in Paris in 1948 who helped draft and signed along with the Chair of the Human Rights Commission, First Lady of the U.S, Eleanor Roosevelt, the **Universal Declaration of Human Rights on December 10th, 1948.**

C. Contributions to the Middle-Eastern Countries

1. Arab Haitians

Arab Haitians are Haitian citizens of Arab descent. In Haiti, there is a sizable number of Haitians that are either of Middle-Eastern ancestry or who trace their origins to Arab descendants. Hadrami and Levantine Arabic ancestry can be found within the Arab Haitian community known in Arabic as *Bilad al-Sham*, primarily Lebanon and Syria.

HAITI: Contributions to the World

The first Arab immigrants to arrive in Haiti reached the shores of the Caribbean country during the middle to late 19th century. During the time, Haiti's business sector was dominated by German and Italian immigrants. Many of them migrated to the countryside where they peddled and were very informal economically speaking. World War I, which took place when Lebanon was part of the Germany-allied Ottoman Empire, triggered a Lebanese migration to the Americas, with Haiti receiving a large number of Lebanese immigrants. Haiti received a group of Palestinian refugees during the 1948 Arab–Israeli War. The country was estimated to have about 257,000 residents of Arab heritage, about 68% of them are mixed-race, mainly mixing with the Haitian mulatto elite.

Arab Haitians are generally considered part of the upper class within Haitian society, yet they maintain their own unique presence separate from the very influential and much larger mixed-race and white Haitian populace. For years, they were shunned by the elite mulatto Haitians because of amicable interaction with the poor masses, their willingness to do business with masses and their inability to speak French. This relationship changed gradually over the years as their prominence grew in Haiti's business sector and consequently, a large percentage of them reside and do business in the capital of Port-au-Prince. Middle-class Arab Haitians often are the owners of many of the city's supermarkets.

2. The Jews in Hayti/Haiti

The history of the Jews in Haiti is a rather long and complex one, as it stretches from the very beginning of the European settlement on the new island.

As of 2013, the Jewish population is around 25, predominately in Port-au-Prince.

In 1492, the first Jew to ever set foot in Hayti was Luis de Torres, an interpreter for Christopher Columbus.

In 1683, the Jews were expelled from Hayti and all of the other French colonies, due to the Code Noir (Black Code), which not only restricted the activities of free Negroes, but forbade the exercise of any religion other than Roman Catholicism (it included a provision that all slaves must be baptized and instructed in the Roman Catholic religion), and in turn ordered all the Jews out of France's colonies. However, despite the Black Code, a limited number of Jews remained in Hayti. Recently, archaeologists have uncovered an ancient synagogue of Crypto-Jews in the city of Jérémie, the only one found on the island.

HAITI: Contributions to the World

In 1915, during the United States occupation of Haiti, roughly 200 Jews lived in Haiti at the time. During the 20 years period of occupation, many Jews left Haiti for the United States and South America. In 1937, Haiti was responsible for saving about 70 Jewish families (an estimated total of up to 300 lives) during the Holocaust (according to the American Jewish Joint Distribution Committee), by issuing passports and visas to Jews escaping Nazi persecution. Some were Austrian Jews, Polish Jews, German Jews, and a few of Romanian Jew and Czech Jewish descent. Haiti played a small, yet critical role in saving Jewish lives during the darkest chapter in the Jewish story. Unfortunately, though, it seems that more Jews were unable to acquire visas to Haiti due to the cost. Professor David Bankier, of the Institute of Contemporary Jewry at the Hebrew University of Jerusalem, said that after 1938, "the cost [of a visa] was outrageous: If you wanted to go to Haiti, you had to pay $5,000." Haiti at the time, was still unfairly paying reparations on an exorbitant debt with interest fees to France after the Haitian Revolution that could have hindered their efforts to continue issuing these visas for free. There were others apart from this bunch who never came to Haiti at all, but from Germany they were given Haitian passports by the Haitian government that allowed them to flee Germany and into other countries.

CHAPTER VI

Summary

Haiti is a small country in size but gigantic in historical dimensions. The people of this country left their prints in the reports of global human rights movements. From the western coast of the African continent to this mountainous island of the Caribbean, the Haitian ancestors have brought with them the pride of the Black race under inhumane conditions.

Enduring one of the worst treatments in the history of mankind, these enslaved individuals found a way to rise to the highest level of bravery and nationalism to change the course of history at the beginning of the nineteenth century, from colonialism to independence and from slavery to freedom.

The traditional history books rarely relate in an objective way the significance of the Haitian experience. They often distort the real historical underpinnings that explain why this country has become weakened, isolated and poor.

HAITI: Contributions to the World

Also, very few history books will convey the historical links between Haiti and its neighbors, as they have always been pioneers in the fight for freedom, independence and social justice.

Haiti and Haitians are proud to be:
- Contributors to the wealth of European nations like Spain and France during the colonial times
- The first modern Black Slaves Republic in the world
- The second independent country in the western hemisphere after the U.S.
- Freedom fighters for the independence of the United States of America in the battle of Savannah, Georgia
- Inspiration for slave revolts and emancipation movements in different countries around the world
- Contributors to the liberation of countries in South and Central America from colonization (The Bolivarian countries: Bolivia, Columbia, Venezuela, Ecuador, Peru, and Panama)

HAITI: Contributions to the World

Moreover, Napoleon's defeat in Hayti was instrumental in his disinterest in the Americas, which led to the Louisiana Purchase by the U.S. in 1803.

CONCLUSION

It is undeniable that Haiti from the time of its revolution in the late 1700s made invaluable contributions to the world. The slave revolt in Hayti on August 21-22, 1791, that started the destruction of the system of slavery, remains one of the greatest gifts to humanity. As recognition of Haiti's fight against slavery, the United Nations Educational, Scientific and Cultural Organization **(UNESCO) has proclaimed August 23rd as the International Day for the Remembrance of the Slave Trade and its Abolition.**

Starting this year **August 23, 2019**, let us celebrate the **International Day of Gratitude towards Haiti** for contributing to make the world a better place for all without slavery, colonization and segregation. "**The entire world owes much to the Haitian Revolution. Our debt to Haiti and the Haitian people has not yet been recognized**" Gwendolyn Midlo Hall.

Haiti, the first modern **Black Slaves Republic** in the world, is rich in cultural and historic values. So let us be aware of it and promote it through this "Compilation of Historical Facts about Haiti's Contributions to the World", by *Jean Paul Jean François.*

APPENDICES

HISTORICAL PICTURES

Toussaint Louverture and Jean-Jacques Dessalines

Toussaint Louverture is the precursor of Haiti's independence and Jean-Jacques Dessalines is the founder of the nation. Jean Jacques Dessalines served under Toussaint Louverture as his lieutenant and, while no one can argue that their styles differed greatly, it is clear that both men were driven by their desire to have all Haitians live as free people in a free country.

After the capture of Toussaint Louverture by the French, Dessalines became the General-in-chief of the revolutionary army; he had liberated the colony of Saint-Domingue from the French and abolished slavery on the land. "La Dessalinienne", our national anthem is attributed to Dessalines.

HAITI: Contributions to the World

The Battle of Vertières

The battle of Vertières took place on November 18, 1803, a legendary day celebrated by Haitians. Dessalines, the commander of about 15,000 soldiers, chose the most intrepid of his generals François Capois to lead the initial attack against the French Army. The most cited and extraordinary episode on this historic day concerned the ardor and incredible luck of General Capois in the heat of the battle. At one point, Capois had his horse shot out from under him. He leapt ahead, sword in the air, urging his men forward. Then his hat was shot off his head and still he kept plunging ahead, with two-thirds of his men already dead or wounded.

Dessalines pulled back Capois and what remained of his unit and ordered another unit under General Gabart into the struggle. Attacks were launched against all blockhouses at the same time to make it impossible for the French to concentrate their fire on any one target. The French were forced to retreat.

After the capitulation of the French, Dessalines ordered Rochambeau and his men to depart from the colony. In less than a month, on January 1, 1804, Dessalines proclaimed the independence of Saint-Domingue and renamed it Hayti after the indigenous Arawak name.

The Battle of Vertières clinched the success of the independence movement. November 18th has since been celebrated as Armed Forces Day in Haiti.

HAITI: Contributions to the World

General Boisrond Tonnerre

On December 31, 1803, the eve of the day that Hayti officially recognizes as Independence Day, Dessalines and the other generals came together in a ceremony to officially proclaim Hayti's independence. During this ceremony, which took place in Gonaives (known as the City of Independence), Boisrond Tonnerre, secretary of the revolutionary army, was chosen by Dessalines to draft the Act of Independence.

HAITI: Contributions to the World

HAITI: Contributions to the World

The Act of Independence of Hayti

The Act of Independence declared the colony of Saint-Domingue independent from France on January 1st, 1804 and renamed it "**Hayti**", the name it had been given by Arawak inhabitants of the island before the arrival of Columbus. The act of independence was drafted by Boisrond Tonnerre and read by Jean-Jacques Dessalines.

It also stated that blacks on this land preferred to die rather than remain slaves "Liberté ou la mort" meaning "Liberty or death".

HAITI: Contributions to the World

La Citadelle Laferrière or Citadelle of Henri Christophe

The largest fortress in the Western hemisphere, the Citadelle of Haiti is located atop a 3,000-foot mountain called Bonnet-à-L'evêque. It was built by King Henri Christophe to protect the interior of Hayti in case the French tried to retake the former colony. So impressive is the fortress, stretched across the mountains peak, with sheer cliffs on three sides and the only point of access subject to withering canon fire, that the United Nations included it in the list of cultural treasures, along with the Acropolis and the Pyramids of Egypt. Haitians proudly consider it as the eighth wonder of the world.

HAITI: Contributions to the World

HAITI: Contributions to the World

The history of the Haitian Flag

- The first flag was created on May 18, 1803 in the Congress of Unity of Blacks and Mulattos held in Arcahaie, a township located about fifty miles North of Port-au-Prince.
- The new constitution of 1805 stated in its general provisions (article 20) that the national colors are black and red.
- After the assassination of Dessalines, there have been many changes of the national flag, from blue and red to black and red depending on the ideology of the regime in power.
- From 1822 to 1844, Jean Pierre Boyer unified Hayti (West) to the Dominican Republic (East) under the blue and red flag.
- In 1964, François Duvalier declared himself President-for-life and adopted the black and red flag.
- The constitution of 1987 (articles 2 and 3) officially reestablished the blue and red flag with the following description: two equal-sized horizontal bands: a blue one on top and a red one underneath. The coat of arms of the Republic shall be placed in the center on a white square.

HAITI: Contributions to the World

The Coat of Arms and the country's motto

The coat of arms of the Republic of Haiti that is placed at the center of the flag along with the motto: "L'union fait la force" [united we're strong] was personally designed by President Alexandre Pétion. The coat of arms of the Republic are a palmette surrounded by the liberty cap, and under the palms, a trophy of weapons with the legend: "L'union fait la force"

HAITI: Contributions to the World

Tribute to Antenor Firmin

Joseph Auguste Anténor Firmin (18 October 1850 – 19 September 1911), better known as **Anténor Firmin**, was a Haitian philosopher, pioneering anthropologist, journalist, and politician. Firmin is best known for his book *De l'égalité des races humaines* (English: "On the Equality of Human Races"), which was published in 1885 as a rebuttal to French writer Count Arthur de Gobineau's work *Essai sur l'inégalité des races humaines* (English: "Essay on the Inequality of Human Races"). Gobineau's book asserted the white race superiority and the inferiority of Blacks and other people of color. Firmin's book argued the opposite, that "all men are endowed with the same qualities and the same faults, without distinction of color or anatomical form. The races are equal". He was marginalized at the time for his beliefs that all human races were equal.

Biography

Joseph Auguste Anténor Firmin was born as the third generation of a post-independent Haiti in a working-class family. Firmin advanced quickly at his studies and started teaching when he was 17. He studied accounting and law. He worked as a clerk for a private business. He quit his clerical position to teach Greek, Latin and French.

He was close to the liberal party, and he started the newspaper "Le Messager du Nord". The political turmoil surrounding the new government of General Salomon forced him into exile in Paris where he served as a diplomat. During this time, he was admitted to the Société d'Anthropologie de Paris where he began writing *De L'Egalite des Races Humaines*.

Firmin attended meetings of the Société as a regular member. But he was silenced by a racialist physical anthropology dominant at the time and due to racism. The transcripts of the Société's deliberations included in the *Mémoires* show that Firmin rose to speak only twice, and on both occasions, he was silenced by racist comments.

Work

Anténor Firmin's major work, *De l'égalité des races humaines (anthropologie positive)* was published in Paris in 1885. Its importance was unrecognized for several decades. The recovered text was translated by Haitian scholar Asselin Charles in 2000. It was published in English as *The Equality of the Human Races (Positivist Anthropology),* 115 years after its original publication. Today he is considered one of the most important contributors to anthropology.

Firmin pioneered the integration of race and physical anthropology and may be the first Black anthropologist. His work was recognized not only in Haiti but also among African scholars as an early work of négritude. He influenced Jean Price-Mars, the founder of Haitian ethnology, and the American anthropologist Melville Herskovits.

Following the ideas of Auguste Comte, Firmin was a stark positivist who believed that the empiricism used to study humanity was a counter to the speculative philosophical theories about the inequalities of races. Firmin sought to redefine the science of Anthropology in his work. He critiqued certain aspects of anthropology, such as craniometry and racialist interpretations of human physical data. He was the first to point out how racial typologies failed to account for the successes of those of mixed race as well as one of the first to state an accurate scientific basis for skin pigmentation.

Of the Equality of Human Races

In his work, *De l'égalité des races humaines* ("Of the Equality of Human Races") published in 1885, Firmin tackles two bases of existing theories on black inferiority to critique Gobineau's *De l'Inégalité des Races Humaines* ("Of the Inequality of Human Races"). On the one hand, Firmin challenges the idea of brain size or cephalic index as a measure of human intelligence and on the other he reasserts the presence of African Blacks in Pharaonic Egypt. He then delves into the significance of the Haitian Revolution of 1804 and ensuing achievements of Haitians such as Léon Audain and Isaïe Jeanty in medicine and science and Edmond Paul in the social sciences. (Both Audain and Jeanty had obtained prizes from the Académie Nationale de Médecine, France)

Founder of Pan-Africanism

Firmin is one of three Caribbean men who launched the idea of Pan-Africanism at the end of the 19th century to combat colonialism in Africa. As a candidate in Haiti's 1902 presidential elections, he declared that the Haitian state should "serve in the rehabilitation of Africa". Along with Trinidadian lawyer Henry Sylvester Williams and fellow Haitian Bénito Sylvain, he was the organizer of the **First Pan-African Conference** which took place in London in 1900. That conference launched the Pan-Africanism movement. W. E. B. Du Bois attended the conference and was put in charge of drafting the general report. After the conference, five pan-African congresses were held in the 20th century, which eventually led to the creation of the African Union.

Firmin was invested in the three main elements of Pan-Africanist: the rejection of the postulate of race inequality, proof that Africans were capable of civilization, and examples of successful Africans producing knowledge in diverse fields. In looking to move away from the biological understanding of race, Firmin's scientific approach was informed by the idea of a Black Egypt as the source of Greek civilization.

Letters from St. Thomas

After a failed bid for presidency in 1902, Firmin was sent to live in exile in St. Thomas. In his last work, *Letters from St. Thomas,* Firmin remaps Haiti in the archipelago of the Americas, outlining its significance to the region. Letters from St Thomas reinforces Firmin's anti-essentialist agenda first displayed in *L'Egalite des Races Humaines*.

Bibliography and Internet Sources

- Revolutionary Freedoms, A history of Survival, Strength and Imagination in Haiti by Cecile Accilien, Jessica Adams and Elmide Méléance

- Celebrating Haitian Heritage: A Teacher's Resource Guide by Bito David

- Encyclopedia Britannica

- The Canadian Encyclopedia

- www.haiti-usa.org/historical

- African American Contributions to the America's Cultures by Jacoby Adeshei Carter

- www.Wikipedia.org, the free encyclopedia

HAITI: Contributions to the World

Reader's Notes

HAITI: Contributions to the World

Reader's Notes

Manufactured by Amazon.ca
Bolton, ON